THE AI PLUG

In this journey of creativity and resilience, I share my story of transformation from a conventional life to a path driven by art and technology. This book captures the pivotal moments of my life, the lessons learned in entrepreneurship, and the power of collaboration, all while giving grace and glory to God.

PUBLISHED BY: Aristeed Brown I

Copyright © 2024 All rights reserved

No part of this publication may be copied, reproduced in any format, by any means, electronic or otherwise, without prior consent from the copyright owner and publisher of this book.

TABLE OF CONTENTS:

TABLE OF CONTENTS: 3
INTRODUCTION: 4
CHAPTER 1: 6
CHAPTER 2: 9
CHAPTER 3: 14
CHAPTER 4: 22
CHAPTER 5: 26
CHAPTER 6: 30
CHAPTER 7: 32
CHAPTER 8: 35
CHAPTER: 9 37
CHAPTER 10: 40
CONCLUSION: 42

INTRODUCTION:

At the crossroads of creativity and cutting-edge technology, a movement was born—one that would redefine how we see the future of art, media, and storytelling. AI Plug: The Journey to Mastery isn't just a chronicle of our accomplishments; it's the story of daring to dream big, leaping into the unknown, and finding triumph on the other side. This is about creating something from nothing, turning setbacks into setups for success, and proving that with the right vision, even the impossible is within reach.

My journey alongside Lee and Majin began with a simple yet powerful decision—to break free from the constraints of the traditional 9-to-5 and embrace a new era fueled by artificial intelligence. In a world where technology can transform imagination into reality, we found ourselves at the forefront of a revolution, driven by a passion to pioneer something the world had never seen.

From sleepless nights spent battling against the limits of AI-generated content to rubbing shoulders with the industry's biggest names, we learned, we grew, and we evolved. What started as a mission to showcase our talents has now blossomed into a movement—a declaration that creativity knows no bounds when paired with the limitless potential of AI.

Through the pages of this book, you'll follow our journey from struggle to success, from unknowns to innovators, from creators to pioneers. It's a testament to grit, determination, and the belief that we could change the game. And we did. The path was anything but smooth, but every hurdle, every challenge, sharpened our skills and prepared us for the future we're building—one where AI isn't just a tool, but a partner in creation.

This is more than a story of mastering technology; it's about mastering ourselves, embracing risk, and carving out a place in a world that's still learning to embrace the power of artificial intelligence. We invite you to experience it with us, to understand that the only limits are the ones we place on ourselves, and to witness firsthand the power of combining passion with innovation. Welcome to the future. Welcome to AI Plug.

CHAPTER 1:

The Beginning of Change

This story begins with the passing of my beloved grandmother, Mrs. Alice Joann Miller. I never anticipated the direction my life would take following her death. Like many families from low-income, poverty-stricken communities, the loss of a pivotal family member often leads to turmoil. In times of grief, true emotions can spiral out of control, exposing fractures within the family unit. It is during these moments that only those who are headstrong, patient, willing to embrace change, and ready to take risks can overcome adversity.

After my grandmother's passing, my sister and I found ourselves at odds with other family members. What baffles me is that my brother, sister, and I were among the few who had stood by her side for years, providing support when she needed it most. It's often the distant relatives who seem to feel the most pain during these times, but I digress.

To set the scene, my grandmother was a sweet, God-fearing woman, particularly in her later years, where her faith shone brightly. However, like many African American families, we faced an overwhelming influence of feminism that complicated traditional roles. The majority of the men on my mother's side are either deceased or incarcerated, leading to a distorted view of masculinity—one that is often perceived as oppressive or toxic.

This narrow-minded perspective has profoundly shaped my worldview. I could never remain silent in the face of the atrocities that have occurred within my family—murders, molestations, sexual abuse, verbal abuse, incest, and more. I choose to speak up rather than be complicit. My grandmother, while loving, often turned a blind eye to some of the most horrific events, and dissenting opinions were met with judgment and ridicule.

Nobody is perfect, and I strive to keep this in mind as I navigate life. It allows me to see people for who they truly are. Whether good or bad, I can discern their true intentions, which helps me move forward thoughtfully. My grandmother's actions, and those of my family members, are not for me—or anyone else—to judge, but rather to learn from. My relationship with my mother's side of the family is bittersweet, characterized by a complex web of emotions and experiences.

My grandmother had four children: my mother, Trelawne, the oldest and the only girl; my eldest uncle, known as "Man"; my uncle Cory; and my youngest uncle, G. Their childhood was marked by dysfunction, abuse, poverty, and immorality, which is a story unto itself. Today, two of her four children have passed away; one is serving a 35-year prison sentence with no chance of parole, while another spent much of his teenage years and early adulthood incarcerated. This leaves us with only one sibling who is physically free, yet mentally, he still carries the scars of institutionalization. Even in his 50s, after serving over a decade in prison, he still identifies as a street man.

The odds have undoubtedly been stacked against us as Black people, but we are not living in the 1960s or 1970s anymore.

We all have choices to make. Blaming our surroundings for our actions, in my opinion, is both childish and unacceptable.

Now that I have set the tone, let's delve into the moment that reopened my eyes and brought that familiar sense of uncertainty rushing back, filling my heart with anxiety. It was a sweltering summer night in early July, just a couple of hours before midnight, when my grandmother fell terribly ill. I can still hear her cries for help, her pain sharp and her agony palpable. Initially, it shook me, but I quickly regained my composure and rushed to her aid.

As I awaited the arrival of the ambulance, it felt as if time had stopped. The air was eerily still, and her hands were cold. I knew time was running out. The blinding red and white lights flashing outside illuminated the room, prompting me to dash outside to flag down the ambulance. I noticed a large firetruck behind it, and three firefighters jumped off, rushing toward me. I led them into the house to help transfer my grandmother from her wheelchair down the stairs and onto the stretcher. It felt like a scene from a movie—my sister, tears streaming down her face, while the entire neighborhood looked on, witnessing my grandmother's final departure from her home.

CHAPTER 2:

DEEPLY ROOTED STRUGGLE

Just days before, she had been grappling with intense shortness of breath and fatigue from the slightest movements. We had been anticipating this hospital visit, even though she was adamantly opposed to going back. At that time, my brother, sister, and I were her primary caregivers, attending to her every need. I vividly remember the irony of seeing many family members—those who later turned on us after her passing—expressing their gratitude for everything we had done for her in their absence.

To my surprise, my uncle, who I had been in touch with before my grandmother's passing, was informed of her condition. I had pleaded with him to visit her, knowing that, as her only surviving child, his presence would mean the world to her.

Uncle G is by no means the worst of my uncles, but he certainly isn't much better, either. His history is shrouded in mystery, and my grandmother specifically requested that we not let him into the house, near her purse, or have access to her car—especially when she wasn't there—because even as a grown man, he was not trustworthy. I remember my mother warning my siblings and me as children that if we had anything we valued, we should hide it whenever Uncle G and his family came to visit. It was chaotic.

After years of urging him to see his terminally ill mother, Uncle G finally made the trip. By then, my grandmother had already been in the hospital for over a month and was actively fighting for her life every day. When he arrived, it was immediately clear that she was overjoyed to see him after such a long time. Not only did he step up for her, but he also stayed in the hospital for a week and a half, tending to her every need—something my brother, sister, and I had consistently done for years.

Having him there was refreshing; it allowed us some relief. With Uncle G's support, we could focus on work, manage bills, and keep up with home maintenance while my grandmother was away.

But, like many situations in my family, the good vibes didn't last. Uncle G began questioning what my sister and I were doing while living at our grandmother's house, which raised a red flag—especially since he hadn't contributed a single dollar to her bills, home renovations, or anything else. Why was he suddenly concerned about our actions when we already had everything under control?

It soon became clear that Uncle G had plans to assume responsibility and ownership of everything in his mother's name after her passing. The first problem with this was that my grandmother had explicitly stated he was entitled to nothing. Second, he attempted to call the shots from two states away, despite never having paid a bill or contributed to the household. Lastly, he had no history of being responsible for anyone or anything, not even his own home.

Naturally, it didn't take long for Uncle G to reveal his true colors. He began asking where my grandmother's purse was because she "needed" it and wanted to know the location of her car keys. His predictability was astounding. I confronted him directly, making it clear that it was unnecessary for him to try to step in at this late stage when we already had everything under control. This infuriated him, and looking back, I understand why—he felt entitled to something that was not his.

He intended to apply pressure, even threatening to send some of his friends to clear out the house. That was a big mistake. Where I'm from, we have a "Stand Your Ground" law, allowing legal retaliation when feeling threatened. I made it abundantly clear that if he or anyone else attempted to come to the house, they would do so at their own risk, which quickly made him reconsider.

I ultimately decided it was best to wash my hands of the entire situation after discovering that my grandmother had been feeding my uncle lies about us. She told him that my sister and I were taking advantage of her, that money was missing, and that we left her to die in the hospital. The hurt and betrayal I felt from this betrayal is beyond measure, even to this day. Yet, my grandmother had always had a knack for stirring up drama, often showing her two-faced nature. It was sobering to realize she did this while on her deathbed.

My decision to leave was unpopular among family members, but at that point, no one had been helping us care for her. How could anyone criticize when they hadn't lifted a finger to assist? Throughout my relatively short life, I've learned many lessons, one of the most important being how to disregard opinions that lack real significance in the grand scheme of things.

Once again, I found myself leaving home without a clear plan—just faith and the determination to make the best of whatever situation I encountered. This motivation made me realize I was worth more than the typical nine-to-five rat race of a temporary staffing agency. I am a man who has worn many hats to get by and has gained experience across various fields.

Writing has always been my first love. Since seventh grade, I've enjoyed using words to captivate readers, and it's this passion that I believe will lead me to success. My first job, however, was at a temporary staffing agency, which began my long, love-hate relationship with the nine-to-five grind, living paycheck to paycheck like many Americans. Fortunately, my extensive experience in such jobs taught me a valuable lesson: you have to take risks to seize opportunities.

Life is about living, and it's a fact that those who are financially free are the ones who truly get to enjoy what life has to offer. To achieve financial freedom, you must genuinely value what you provide to others and be willing to be of service. While being used often carries a negative connotation, people forget there's a significant difference between being used and being misused.

Before my grandmother passed, I would travel over 60 miles a day after my regular work hours to drop off a good friend who was battling a DUI. If I hadn't been there for him, he wouldn't have been able to keep his job or stay on top of his bills. He was grateful then, and he still is, as are his family, who often remind me of how much of an asset I was to him. I was being used for rides, and he was helping refill my gas tank weekly.

One lesson people could really benefit from is the power of teamwork and the mutual benefits it can bring. It costs nothing to do what you believe is right without overextending yourself. That kindness allowed me to have a place to live when I needed it most. No situation is ever perfect, but it's always about how you make the most of it. I was incredibly grateful for a place to sleep, but my allergies to cats made couch surfing uncomfortable—especially since there were 12 cats in the home I had just moved into. As a result, I often found myself sleeping in my car, still going to my temp agency job every day, moving nowhere fast.

Eventually, my buddy, whose heart is as big as the sun, insisted that I find somewhere more comfortable to sleep. Before I could refuse, he cleared out his shed for me, and just like that, I had the ultimate bachelor pad! RGB LED lights, a premium studio-grade sound system, and a large 52-inch TV—complete with bottles and bottles of liquor everywhere, though to be honest, I'm not much of a drinker.

You would've thought I had it made, given how secure I appeared, even while not living right. I effectively deluded myself to autopilot through the daily grind of what was, in reality, insanity. Sure, it was fun having friends over after hanging out at the beach bars, playing games, and watching movies, but there was an itch I couldn't scratch—a deep, underlying hunger for more from life.

CHAPTER 3:

A New Partnership

With each passing day, another opportunity to make a change slips by. Being stuck in the nine-to-five rat race—working a myriad of jobs through a temporary staffing agency—had me living in a zombie-like state of mind. Over my relatively short life, I've held more than 1,000 different jobs. This year alone, I transitioned from electrician to janitor, vacuum tester to forklift operator. Yet, no matter what I did, one overarching truth remained: no job will ever set you free.

My resentment towards work deepened after my paychecks were garnished for child support. Since my child was born, I haven't received a single income tax return, and I found myself barely scraping by with same-day and weekly pay jobs. Drowning in problems, I refused to give up or blame anyone else for my circumstances—they were my problems, after all. I firmly believe in self-accountability; we are ultimately responsible for our own well-being and the outcomes of our choices.

At times, I hated my living situation—there was no privacy, no say, no control. I accepted this as my life until it wasn't anymore. I've mastered the art of gratitude, understanding that demonstrating appreciation not only uplifts others but also fosters meaningful connections. To become an asset, you must provide value; sometimes, just being present is invaluable, depending on the circumstances. Soak up knowledge and never become complacent. These are some of the principles I live by to stay humble, grounded, and well-rounded.

No single situation can make or break you. Once you adopt this mindset, you'll begin to see the world from a bird's-eye view. I finally decided to take my future into my own hands at the very next opportunity.

Living in the shed humbled me in many ways. Each night, I had the pleasure of looking up at the ceiling, watching bugs crawl about. I knew I was alive, but I wasn't truly living. I felt trapped, yet in my mind, I believed there was a way out—even if I had no clue what that might be. Still, I spoke positivity into my life. Some might say I was living in denial; maybe I was. Yet, confidence seeped through my pores at the mere thought of things changing for the better. In theory, this mindset should effectively shift one's reality based on perception. One day, mind hacks will surely be a thing—mark my words.

I started engaging more on social media, connecting with like-minded people. I began to build a small following by making others laugh and sharing my music to get their reactions. For those who know me, music is my passion, but I'm well aware of how oversaturated the industry is. I needed to find a way to stand out.

Despite my growing online presence, I was still stuck in dead-end jobs, barely making ends meet. It was time for a change; I was mentally prepared, but not financially ready. Then, one day, it happened like clockwork. My roommates wanted to hold a house meeting after dinner. They were friends of a friend, and while I hadn't known them well initially, I soon realized they were great people who always looked out for one another.

The big news was that my roommate's girlfriend had landed a unique job, and they would soon be moving out. You could hear their excitement and see the joy in their faces; it was evident they had worked hard for this moment long before I arrived. We popped a couple of bottles and celebrated their achievement around the bonfire.

The next day, my buddy, the homeowner, informed me that while he was thrilled for our roommates, their move would tighten our finances. The timing couldn't have been worse—property management had just raised the lot rent that month. We were now facing nearly a thousand dollars each in monthly rent. There was no way I could justify paying upwards of nine hundred dollars a month for my current living situation.

Unsure of what to do or where to turn, I received a random phone call from an acquaintance I had met at a bar just two months earlier. As random as it seemed, I reminded myself that nothing is truly random; God makes no mistakes and orchestrates everything for a reason.

Unaware of the door I had just opened by answering the phone, I couldn't have fathomed how much my life was about to change. On the other end was a man named Lee, whose confidence and ambition seemed to seep through the line. He passionately described a recent "spiritual awakening" that had clearly shaken him up; his eagerness to share this profound realization was palpable. As he scrambled to communicate his experience, he came off as scatterbrained, unhinged, and at times, even a bit crazy. But I've learned that some of the most brilliant minds often belong to the most unconventional people. When you create a safe space for them to express themselves, challenge their thoughts, and help them organize their ideas, one of two things will happen: they will either accept and flourish, or resist and crash.

Lee was the loud and proud extrovert I had met at a hole-in-the-wall Japanese anime-style bar, but there was something notably different about him this time. His empathy and willingness to listen were evident. When we first met on the bar's back patio, I had stepped out for a smoke and found him surrounded by at least five people. He was animatedly explaining real estate strategies and how to invest for a solid return on investment. His words flowed with clarity and conviction, using terminology I had never heard before. It was captivating and informative, and I found myself drawn in.

Either he was an actor or a genius; he reminded me of those charismatic figures you see in video commercials—people who make you want to buy whatever they're selling. His rapid-fire delivery was almost overwhelming, yet you could tell he genuinely believed in what he was saying. In essence, Lee was looking for partners to help invest in his mission: making homes and homebuying more affordable for future generations of Americans. His passion was compelling enough to inspire me to introduce myself and, before leaving to head back inside, to get his contact information.

When I sense someone is genuine, I aim to convey my intentions by being open, clear, assertive, and a touch vulnerable. This approach helps to foster trust. One of my strategies is simply introducing myself by my first name. My name is unique, and I've learned to embrace it; I often receive either praise or ridicule for it. I've long since outgrown my insecurities and accepted that the world owes us no understanding. Instead, it's our responsibility to earn respect through our actions and how we treat others. Perception is reality, and you only get one chance to make a first impression. So, be the example you want to see and carve out your own path in life.

Choosing who I reveal my first name to has opened my mind to the different reactions from various types of people. For instance, my family embodies the modern Black experience, often mixed with a sprinkle of ignorance. As a result, those with a lower level of understanding tend to ridicule what they don't comprehend. It can be amusing to see people visibly thrown off; some even try to give me nicknames, while others outright say they "just can't say all that." Navigating these differences can be challenging, but I digress.

Now, back to my first meeting with Lee. As I approached him, he immediately gave me his full attention, reaching out for a handshake. I reciprocated, and he greeted me with confidence and respect. Leaning in, I clearly enunciated each syllable of my name directly into his ear. He responded with an approving look and a strong nod—only to mispronounce my name. It was an epic fail that I find hilarious in retrospect. I corrected him, yet he still struggled to get it right. To save us both some time, I introduced myself by my nickname instead.

Life has certainly shaped me in interesting ways, to say the least. Unsurprisingly, Lee kept everyone entertained that night, and we all learned a lot about him. He maintained direct eye contact as he spoke, leaving a lasting impression on me.

The call that changed everything began with Lee recounting a daunting story about a recent trip to Colorado. He had made the journey for a woman he had been seeing—someone he had grown to admire, respect, and appreciate deeply. After months of effort, he finally got her to let her guard down, and he was ready to declare his love. Driven by anticipation, he traveled over eight hours to spend New Year's with what he hoped would be his one true love.

Unfortunately, things didn't unfold as he had envisioned. The woman flaked on him, revealing her struggles with past heartbreaks and her fear of falling in love again. It was clear she hadn't fully healed from her trauma and couldn't trust a man. Lee had given his all, and to be let down like this felt selfish on her part. Crushed, heartbroken, and confused, he realized he needed to clear his mind and find a place to rest after such an emotional rollercoaster.

As he drove, daylight began to fade. Just then, off the side of the highway, a small, ragged-looking hotel appeared almost out of nowhere.

As Lee pulled up to the hotel entrance, he realized he was in a small, sketchy town, dimly lit with barely any streetlights. A group of homeless people seemed to appear out of nowhere, roaming the streets. Just as he parked, one man waved him down and asked for spare change. Like many these days, Lee didn't carry cash, but he did have an extra medical marijuana joint he could spare. The man's surprise turned into gratitude as he happily accepted the offer, praising Lee as he walked away.

Feeling proud of his small act of kindness, Lee headed toward the lobby. After checking in and paying for his room, he received his key and went off to recharge. However, as he stepped outside, he noticed the homeless man was now standing by his car with another guy who looked just as down on his luck. With a big smile, the man asked Lee if he wanted to hang out and smoke with them.

Lee humbly declined, explaining that he'd had a long day and needed to rest. In an instant, the men's friendly demeanor shifted to visible anger. They stormed off in the direction Lee needed to go to reach his room, raising the hairs on the back of his neck.

Cautiously, Lee made his way to his room, focusing intently on his surroundings. Once inside, he took a much-needed hot shower and ate a comforting meal, finally ready to call it a night—until a loud, frantic banging at the door shattered the silence.

Jolting out of bed to answer the door, Lee was confronted by the same homeless man he had given the pre-rolled joint to. The man was screaming obscenities, accusing Lee of lacing the joint with fentanyl. He claimed his friend was having a seizure after taking a few drags, and if Lee didn't want to go to jail, he needed to help get his friend to a hospital.

Visibly shaken and confused, Lee reluctantly agreed to help. As they approached the hotel room, the man held the door open for Lee to enter first, but Lee was too smart for that. Insisting the man go in first, he followed cautiously. As he stepped into the dimly lit room, Lee's heart sank; there were at least seven other dark figures inside—way more people than he had been led to believe. Whatever was happening here couldn't be good.

Instinctively, he stepped back, closed the door, and bolted back to his own room. Grabbing his bag, he quickly dropped the keys in the hotel drop box and jumped into his car, swerving out of the parking lot and narrowly escaping what felt like a dangerous setup.

Lee drove until he reached the next big city, where the streets were illuminated and bustling with life. He recounted how he had met an older couple who owned a karaoke bar, forging a bond with them after sharing the harrowing tale of his trip. That night at the bar was the only time Lee felt truly at peace amidst the chaos of his life. He connected with many kind-hearted people, and when the New Year's Ball dropped, he experienced a profound spiritual awakening.

Before he left, the couple pulled him aside and, out of genuine kindness, offered him VIP treatment for life whenever he returned to their city.

One of the worst experiences of Lee's life had just transformed into one of the best. With a new outlook and understanding, this journey would prove to be one of the most significant trips of his life. As he drove home, something unexpected happened. A song began to play—one that wasn't even in his playlist.

This song was captivating, ethereal, and soul-gripping. It enveloped Lee in a whirlwind of heartache, agony, pain, and triumph all at once. Who was this artist whose voice pierced his soul so profoundly? He discovered, to his shock, that this mega superstar had tragically passed away four years prior.

Overwhelmed by an intense wave of sorrow and despair, Lee pulled over to the side of the road, tears streaming down his face. It didn't make any sense; how could he feel such a deep emotional reaction to someone he hadn't even known existed until now? He felt utterly destroyed, empty, as if he were sharing in the world's collective grief over this artist's passing.

In that moment of heartbreak, Lee realized that this artist's music resonated with him in a way nothing ever had before. This was the spark of something far greater than he could have ever imagined. A profound urge to create music welled up within him. Though he had never written a single lyric in his life, the weight of inspiration began to settle in his heart, and then... he started to write.

CHAPTER 4:

Diving into AI

Time knows no filter, no beginning or end; life will unfold whether you're ready or not. For me, life "happened" when it was time to plan yet another move. I couldn't wait any longer after my roommates had left; I needed to start searching soon.

Interestingly, after Lee and I began to talk on the phone, he opened up more about his living situation. He mentioned that he would eventually need a roommate to help cover his mortgage. He also shared his newfound love for music and songwriting, eager to know my thoughts on his work. Given my long history with music, I was excited to hear what he had created, but I preferred to listen in person rather than over the phone. We set up a day to hang out and really talk.

On the day of our meeting, I was covered in sawdust from working at the lumber yard. After nine hours of work, I was exhausted but ready to go. Lee lived in a newer housing development, and his area wasn't yet in the GPS system, so he suggested I look out for the house number instead. When I arrived, I saw him wave me in with a friendly smile.

Meeting up was great; I was impressed by how well he kept his home. We settled in to talk about everything—his spiritual awakening, Jessie, the blonde-haired, blue-eyed love that got away, women in general, our pasts, and our shared experiences. It was clear we had formed a bond, realizing that despite our different backgrounds, we had more in common than we initially thought.

Being open, honest, and accepting criticism are essential for understanding any situation. Discernment and respect are equally important; life has taught me the value of tact for self-preservation. When someone shares their story, it's crucial to listen actively. I trusted Lee without reservation, and from that day on, I saw him as both a friend and a colleague. I didn't leave until around midnight, fully aware I had to be up for work at 5 a.m. After making it home, I showered and crashed into bed.

It was time to make the move, this time into a completely new situation in an unfamiliar area. Lee and I had agreed I would move in; his house functioned more as a business hub than a home. After the daily grind of my nine-to-five job, I'd return to engage in deep conversations about music. Lee was genuinely impressed by my musical skills, while I admired his fresh, unique songwriting that reflected his personal journey. I've listened to enough music to know that every song carries meaning, even the so-called "bad" ones. If a song has an abstract or unconventional message, it deserves to be heard; if it's meant to resonate, it will.

Lee's background in IT was remarkable. His advanced knowledge of computer engineering and programming was evident in his impressive setup: multiple monitors, a high-end gaming chair, and headphones. He could type at lightning speed while maintaining eye contact and ensuring his words were mostly correct. It was clear he was in a league of his own, and I was eager to learn his efficiency. With at least six or seven years of experience ahead of me, I entered this situation with maybe 5% of the computer skills I needed. But I saw this as my chance to learn something new.

After moving in, we dedicated ourselves to leveraging AI to our advantage. We began to expand our minds together, challenging each other's ideas, and forging a shared goal: to master the internet with Artificial Intelligence.

As a musician, artist, or content creator, offering special, exclusive, and custom content is essential for engaging your fans and enhancing your brand. Given my financial constraints, I couldn't invest in nice clothes, expensive jewelry, fast cars, or a cameraman to capture it all. So, we turned to AI and its generative capabilities. At that time, I was somewhat familiar with ChatGPT but knew little about the vast potential of Midjourney. Discovering the ability to generate images through Midjourney's AI chatbot on Discord was a game changer.

Lee introduced the idea of creating visualizer videos for his music, suggesting we first test the waters with his tracks before collaborating on my own. I was all in! The thought of creating anything we envisioned, with imagination as our only limit, was exhilarating. Crafting individual prompts felt more like coding than anything else; we learned to include image descriptions, settings, tags, camera angles, lighting cues, styles, and character references. Some prompts stretched to half a page, but we persisted until we generated images that aligned with our vision.

Little did we know, we were paving the way for one of the most innovative and vital careers that would soon be essential for creative expression. Digital brand awareness, marketing, product promotion, and the ability to creatively advertise were right at our fingertips. In three to five years, what we were doing would set the standard for artists, musicians, and content creators everywhere. Embracing the role of an AI Engineer is not just an option; it's the future.

We had finally begun to grasp the incredible potential of AI, using it to create some of the most intriguing images we'd ever seen. From a Dragon Ball Z x Jet Set Radio crossover themed rap video to Samurai-inspired Star Wars visuals, if we could dream it, we could create it! Lee was remarkably efficient in his work; he would compartmentalize his projects and juggle multiple tasks simultaneously. After about three weeks of collaborating, I was able to keep pace and really catch on.

We also discovered a website called Runway ML, which allowed us to animate images—a true game changer! What would have required an entire team and months, if not years, to complete now took us just days. Learning to meticulously brush stroke each individual movement, akin to applying paint, and running multiple images through Runway's Motion Generator was a daunting yet exhilarating task. Most people wouldn't willingly put themselves through such a labor-intensive process, but we were committed to mastering it.

What we were doing felt revolutionary. The results we achieved by integrating this technology into our everyday creative workflow were mind-blowing. It baffled me that AI wasn't universally recognized for its power or widely accepted for what it could accomplish. However, we were not alone in seeing the value of this technology.

We decided to become affiliates for a popular live streaming service to generate some income. Lee streamed throughout the day, showcasing his AI projects and connecting with curious viewers fascinated by his work. After I got home from work, we conducted music reactions and discussed various topics on our podcast in the evenings. This consistent effort became our foolproof plan, and we stuck with it for three months straight.

Becoming an affiliate on the live-streaming platform was no easy feat. My buddy Lee dedicated at least two months to streaming every single day for 12 to 16 hours. It was incredible to witness his relentless drive toward his goals. Gradually, one viewer turned into two, two into four, and so on. Once his channel bloomed, it really took off. Our unique dynamic—his extroverted personality paired with my laid-back demeanor—created an entertaining synergy. We focused on our personal projects, conducted music reactions, and engaged with other artists while promoting our AI engineering to live viewers.

CHAPTER 5:

The Dream Client

Through this journey, we connected with amazing people from all over the world—shoutout to Uganda, Saudi Arabia, London, and New Zealand! I truly enjoyed the conversations I had with folks from these countries during our livestreams. As we cultivated new relationships online, one fateful day, a live streamer named MajinBuu joined Lee's stream and requested his reaction to one of his videos. Majin immediately caught Lee's attention, as we both considered him the best villain in the entire Dragon Ball Z series!

Unfortunately, I was tied up in the nine-to-five grind at the time, so I missed Lee's initial interaction with Majin. However, Lee later shared how impressed he was with Majin's work. Majin had been using Midjourney for about nine months and was uploading videos to YouTube that garnered tens of thousands, even hundreds of thousands, of views. His content was fluent, dynamic, and captivating.

Seeing someone successfully achieve what we were aiming for was incredibly inspiring. To our surprise, Majin expressed genuine interest in our work and wanted to share his knowledge with us to help elevate our content. It was refreshing to encounter someone willing to teach without a paywall, so we were eager to soak up everything Majin had to offer.

Not only was Majin creating his own personal projects, but he also had a professional client who was paying him to produce industry-level pop music videos for their group. This was a clear signal to me that I should invest my time into this, as he was operating at a high level, proving that I could do it too. Motivated, I was eager to soak up as much knowledge as possible.

Now we arrive at the moment that defines a true hustler—a real go-getter's test. It's that unforeseen moment that can either make or break you. Are you willing to risk it all and remain steadfast when your back is against the wall? Many claim they want change, but do they seize opportunities when they arise? While I haven't been on this earth long, I know that if I'm still doing what I was a year or two ago, I'm not progressing. I aim to be the example I want to see, leading the way toward financial freedom and breaking generational barriers.

Fate knocked at my door when life had been fruitful until then. My nine-to-five job was starting to show signs of false promise, and everything felt steady—until I began experiencing car trouble. I don't know if you've felt the inconvenience of being without reliable transportation, but it hit me suddenly, and I was under immense pressure. I faced an uphill battle: I needed to work to pay my bills and now also needed to fix my car. With my home far from anyone who could give me rides, I was in a tough spot.

This was a pivotal moment for me. I realized that life shouldn't be about waking up every day to clock in at a job where I could never earn more than my allotted pay, where my position felt expendable, and where I had to tolerate a lot of immaturity. The idea of breaking free from that routine felt like a dream come true.

Aristeed Brown I

My car officially broke down on a Thursday evening, and my supervisor generously allowed me to take Friday off and the whole weekend to sort out my transportation. But as kind as that gesture was, I knew I didn't have nearly enough money to fix my car and no way to get to work that Monday. I had to let go of my stress and worries and just allow life to unfold.

Hindsight is always twenty-twenty, and reflecting on this situation proves that saying to be true because of what happened the very next day. Majin received a message from his sister, letting him know that he had been contacted by a famous singer and well-known actor who wanted him to create a music video. His sister, who worked as a handler for this celebrity, discovered that he was eager to explore the capabilities of AI. Once she learned that he was searching for the best person to help bring his music video to life, she made sure to showcase some of Majin's work to him.

Apparently, the celebrity had fired every AI engineer he knew to find the right fit, and upon discovering Majin, he wanted to set up a meeting as soon as possible. It felt surreal—almost too good to be true—but it was happening. Majin had just completed his first project for an industry client and had the bandwidth to take on another before his next obligation, so he asked Lee and me to join him on this exciting venture. The timing couldn't have been better; we had a superstar client, and the potential to elevate our work into the spotlight was thrilling.

By this point, Lee and I had only been working with AI for about three and a half months, so the chance to showcase our work to millions was incredible. Majin employed various tools and platforms to create his videos, so he made sure we were all on the same page. He generously sent us hundreds of dollars to cover any accounts and add-ons we needed to execute the project. Not only was Majin a valuable friend, but he also earned our respect for his willingness to invest in us. He appreciated our eagerness to learn and the fact that we genuinely listened when he shared tips and insights. It was clear he would be our mentor, and we welcomed his expertise.

However, there was a crucial detail worth noting: when Majin accepted the celebrity as a client, he agreed to work without any form of payment. This would prove to be a significant mistake, as you'll see later.

CHAPTER 6:

Building Together

Now, time was running out for me. It was Sunday, and I faced a critical decision. My car still hadn't been fixed, and I had to return to work the next day. I was in an unfamiliar part of town, with no knowledge of the local bus routes, and I doubted I could even find a bus stop nearby. If I lost my job, I wouldn't be able to pay my bills or my child support, which could lead to losing my license and possibly a warrant for my arrest. My future felt uncertain, and I was genuinely down in the dumps.

My back was against the wall, and I was on the brink of insanity. I refused to let everything I had worked for be in vain! I wasn't ready to give up, but I knew I had to regain control of my situation by any means necessary. As I started searching for bus routes on my phone, there was a knock at my door. It was Lee. He sensed my energy had shifted, even though I hadn't said a word, and he was genuinely concerned.

I decided to seize the moment and poured out my worries, concerns, and possible solutions. As I listed my problems, I noticed a look of confusion on his face. Once I finished, Lee said, "Dude, let's build this company together." He explained that if I stayed home to help him, it would double our productivity. Before we met Majin, we had already achieved so much: creating our own visualizers, producing videos, and becoming affiliates on one of the biggest livestream platforms. My nine-to-five job was a barrier to our success.

"I'm going to put my trust in you; I believe in you," I replied. At that moment, I felt like a free man. I don't know if it's appropriate to compare this feeling to my ancestors being freed from slavery, but it was a profound shift. For the first time in my life, I had bet on myself. I had been a part-time entrepreneur, but I realized that without both feet in, nothing would truly work.

Lee had a drive and ambition unlike anyone I knew. He believed in himself, and I did too. There's something refreshing about trusting someone who is determined to succeed, no matter the odds. We agreed that our first official client would be a well-known artist and actor with hundreds of millions of followers on Instagram. Even though we wouldn't be getting paid, the potential "clout" and recognition were payment enough in our eyes.

CHAPTER 7:

The Project from Hell

However, I must be honest about our experience with the client—it was a rollercoaster ride. One moment, we received praise and were told we were doing "God's work"; the next, we faced complaints, ungratefulness, and disrespect, including calling Majin "Master Chief" a woman. It felt incredibly disrespectful, and there were times when it seemed like our efforts were going unappreciated.

Looking back, the situation didn't end positively. There were tensions between the client and Majin, unanswered questions, assumptions, and significant miscommunication.

The project was gargantuan in scope. I still remember Majin admitting halfway through that we might have bitten off more than we could chew. We had to create at least fifteen unique settings from the ground up, complete with a cinematic intro and outro, AI-generated voices for distinct characters, special sound effects, storytelling elements, and flashbacks spanning different time periods. All of this while featuring over one hundred of the most iconic celebrities and superstars, both alive and deceased, who represented black excellence and embodied what our culture is and should continue to be.

The client had a grand vision—one filled with greatness, excellence, luxury, pain, beauty, and grandeur. Our first step was to understand each pivotal moment and capture the unique experiences that each scene conveyed. We focused on style, color, atmosphere, and even how to make historical figures seem natural alongside people they'd never met. This was my initiation into becoming a superstar in my own right. My ancestors were effectively opening the door to my success. I knew I had to represent each featured individual with respect and dignity.

Lee and Majin often turned to me for input on character design, clothing, and whether actions aligned with personalities based on my research. For instance, Huey P. Newton wouldn't be the bartender, and Stevie Wonder wouldn't be the chauffeur. I haven't even touched on the technical challenges that Majin and Lee faced throughout the project. We learned about style references and style weight, which dictated how prominently a particular style was featured.

In one scene, we placed a lion in the VIP section of a club, adorned with diamonds, rubies, sapphires, platinum, and gold jewelry. The idea of having young Coretta Scott King, Whitney Houston, Richard Pryor, and Duke Ellington all in one place was surreal. Each character had their own unique reference code, with variations in outfits and camera angles. Our goal was to blow our client's mind with our creativity—and we succeeded.

I vividly recall one Friday afternoon when Lee, Majin, and I were on a call with the client. Majin had included us on the call so we could hear everything and truly grasp that we were working with a mega superstar. This particular day, the client was at a recording studio session, and for some reason, Majin was on the phone with him there. To our astonishment, the client was sobbing uncontrollably. Confused, Lee and I exchanged glances and burst into laughter. "Is he crying or...?" Lee couldn't even finish his thought as we howled. Thank goodness we were muted!

It turned out the client needed to cry to get into the right mindset for a song, but the irony of the moment was just too much. You had to be there to fully appreciate how hilarious it was.

CHAPTER 8:

Climbing the Mountain

Majin likened the process of generating and animating images to an adventure. It began in the jungle, where we found ourselves washed ashore—the start of our journey typing prompts, codes, tags, and special links to generate images. Next, we reached the plateau. After generating over five thousand images, it was time to craft our characters. We needed images from every angle—front, back, left, and right—to create three-dimensional models of our main characters.

Once we had our characters, we inserted each one into the specific scenes according to the story. We had traversed the vast green plateau and now faced the mountains. This marked the beginning of the long grind—upscaling our images to the highest quality. This was a time-consuming task, as AI often struggles with limbs, especially fingers. The upscaling software corrected each image, but sometimes unusable images slipped through the cracks, requiring meticulous attention.

Reaching the mountain's peak brought both a sense of accomplishment and peace. However, we soon spotted the ocean and a bustling ship port in the distance—civilization awaited us. The descent was treacherous, leading us into the desert. Looking back, animating that project felt like traversing the Sahara. We were at the mercy of older technology, making Runway ML a real challenge. Generating animations was less like wishing in a well and more like hoping on a monkey's paw; we crossed our fingers and prayed to God that any animated image would come out at least halfway decent. Characters morphed into sofas, consumed microphones, and popped in and out of existence. It was undoubtedly the worst part of the process, and even now, it's astonishing we managed to pull it off.

After navigating through our five hundred and eleventh mirage, we finally discovered the real oasis. It was time to cleanse ourselves from the harsh desert experience and let the water flow as we patiently moved through the editing and storyboarding process. This alone took at least four days and proved to be a daunting challenge. Meanwhile, Majin and the client often clashed over the visual direction of certain scenes. Some characters didn't meet expectations, and the client was visibly displeased. Despite the tension, Majin released the video.

By this point, Majin and Lee had put in twelve to sixteen-hour workdays, while I had contributed six to nine hours a day. The project was costly, with Majin spending nearly eighty percent of his bank account on website subscriptions, credits, and replenishments across various platforms. This project drained us all; it was the most grueling three and a half weeks of our lives. But we completed the job—and quickly! Most projects of this magnitude would take sixty days or more to finish. We were proud of our work, but according to Majin, he was done caring about the client's opinion. "We worked and we worked DAMN HARD at that!" he declared, making it clear he wouldn't be taking on any more work for "that guy again.

CHAPTER: 9

THE TURNING POINT

I felt undoubtedly conflicted. While I understood Majin's frustration, I also recognized the opportunities he had missed to address the situation. The client had no idea about the immense effort and work we had put into the project. Miscommunication loomed large between them, and neither could maintain a cool head to navigate the conflict. Up until that point, the client wasn't even aware that Lee and I were involved in the project.

It was time for a serious huddle between Majin, Lee, and me. We couldn't leave things as they were. I reminded Majin that he had agreed to work without payment before Lee and I joined in, which was the first and most significant mistake. As a business, we had to accommodate our clients, regardless of our feelings. I understood all too well why the client was displeased; any pushback on a video meant to represent my vision would upset me too.

Moreover, the client came from a background of poverty, where every dollar mattered. I felt that once he truly grasped the hard work, time, and dedication we had invested, we might receive some form of compensation for our efforts. We needed to ensure that if things went off the rails, it wouldn't be due to our missteps.

After discussing our perspectives, we all agreed to approach the client from a different angle. In business, reputation is everything; it precedes you at every turn. We resolved to remain professional, assertive, honest, confident, concise, and considerate.

A couple of days passed before we heard from the client, and it was good news. Majin informed us that the client wanted to hop on a call with Lee and me to personally thank us for all our work. Although he didn't feel fully connected to the project, the reaction it garnered on social media was, in my opinion, payment enough. I wished I could reveal the iconic figures who had reacted, reshared, and been floored by what we created. People had genuinely connected with the project. At that moment, it became clear that while the mind behind the creation might be artificial, the heart infused in it was very real. You can't deny a feeling, even if you tried.

Together, Lee and I informed Majin that we had agreed to accept the client's phone call. This was a significant moment, as we had been preparing for weeks, meticulously planning how to communicate everything we wanted to express. We discussed how we would introduce ourselves, share our experiences, outline areas for improvement, and remain open to criticism. While neither of us were die-hard fans of the client, we certainly respected their work, which had reached millions globally. We understood we were speaking with someone who had enjoyed a successful career for decades.

To play devil's advocate, many might argue that it doesn't matter who someone is or what they've accomplished; everyone is human. Yet, it's undeniable that celebrities occupy a different social status. This nuance between idolization and expressing genuine appreciation for creativity is essential. While we prepared for the conversation, nothing could truly equip us for the three-and-a-half-hour discussion that followed.

It was one of the most pivotal conversations of my life. We covered everything—from the project itself to our personal stories and future aspirations. The client was vocal about the importance of our work; we were truly pushing the needle forward. We learned about how Majin met the client and their plans to collaborate in the future. The dialogue was intellectually compelling and thought-provoking, culminating in the client persuading us to undertake a top-secret project for other high-profile individuals. Majin and Lee were on board, but I was concerned; there hadn't been any talk of compensation, and the rush to embrace this new venture felt hasty.

The client outlined their ideas and asked for a brief concept video for their colleagues. Majin and Lee swiftly created it, but the response was less than favorable. When projects are rushed, corners are cut, and the result lacks the depth that connects creators to their work. My colleagues took the criticism too personally and decided to quit working for what they deemed an "egotistical person."

I had mentally checked out when the client pushed for the new project, but not for the same reasons. I knew how crucial it was to conduct business properly and communicate professionally. While I understood my colleagues' frustrations, I was tired of repeating myself. Eventually, Majin informed the client that we wouldn't do any more work for them, and after that, we hadn't heard from the client for months. It was a challenge to reach the right people to ensure the project was posted properly on social media, which felt like an odd task for us.

Ironically, Majin had previously shared that the client had advised him to stand his ground and say no, claiming that doing so would elevate his value. Yet, having just said no, it seemed that advice didn't apply in this case. However, I could say the client was correct about our collective value increasing. At this point, my team and I had collaborated with far more iconic figures in the industry and met many incredible people globally, all thanks to our work with AI.

CHAPTER 10:

A NEW ERA

Lee, Majin, and I have gained invaluable insights into the world of entrepreneurship. We've learned that being open, honest, and transparent is essential; our reputations are always at stake. As we continue to carve out our niches, our stock has never been higher. Each month, our income has steadily increased, thanks to investors who recognize the unique value we bring with AI.

Our journey began with a dream of freedom—freedom from the monotonous nine-to-five grind that felt like a never-ending cycle. I'm grateful for my colleagues and the immense growth we've achieved together. Majin found his stride, garnering nearly half a million views for his innovative AI-generated mini-series. Lee created a captivating video for one of his favorite artists, which was showcased at a live concert attended by over one hundred thousand fans.

I've been fortunate to secure a recording deal with a reputable independent label, backed by a major label, just six months into pushing my music. Remarkably, our first client returned, praising our progress and cheering us on.

We know there's still much work ahead, but we're ready for the challenge. I proudly stake my claim as one of the few pioneering AI-generated content in innovative ways. Even as you read this, we are tirelessly working to build the future, harnessing the brilliance of artificial intelligence fueled by our passion and love for what we do.

CONCLUSION:

THE ART OF RESILIENCE AND INNOVATION

As I stand at the crossroads of art, technology, and entrepreneurship, I realize that this journey has been far more than just a pursuit of creative expression. It has been a testament to resilience, faith, and the relentless drive to push boundaries in ways I never imagined. From the struggles of breaking away from the nine-to-five grind to the sleepless nights spent learning, failing, and trying again, every step has shaped not only my career but my character.

The truth is, we live in a time where technology and creativity are no longer separate worlds; they are converging at an unprecedented pace. Artificial intelligence, once seen as merely a tool, has become an integral part of the creative process, allowing us to explore new depths of imagination, to tell stories in ways that transcend the limitations of our physical abilities. Yet, no matter how advanced the AI, it is driven by human intent, passion, and heart. The mind behind the machine may be artificial, but the emotions fueling it are very real.

Through this process, I have learned that creating art—whether it's music, visual storytelling, or digital content—demands more than technical skill. It requires an unwavering dedication to your vision, the courage to embrace new challenges, and the humility to learn from every misstep along the way. I've faced clients who were difficult, projects that seemed impossible, and moments where giving up felt like the easiest option. But it's in those moments that I found the most growth.

Majin, Lee, and I have created something extraordinary, not just for ourselves, but for a community of artists, creators, and innovators who are ready to redefine what's possible. Our success isn't measured only by the projects we've completed or the accolades we've received, but by the lives we've touched, the dreams we've inspired, and the culture we've helped preserve and propel forward.

The future is limitless, and the canvas is vast. Together, with the power of AI and human creativity intertwined, we are pioneering a new era. And as we continue to build, learn, and grow, I carry with me the lessons of resilience, the importance of integrity, and the faith that everything happens for a reason. This journey is far from over. In fact, it has only just begun.

In the end, it's not about the fame, the followers, or even the fortune. It's about freedom—the freedom to create, to dream, and to forge a path that others thought was impossible. It's about leaving a legacy, not just for ourselves, but for the generations who will come after us. This is our story, and it's only the beginning.

www.ingramcontent.com/pod-product-compliance
Lightning Source LLC
Chambersburg PA
CBHW030518220526
45464CB00006B/2856